SPEAKING FREELY
PART II

Audra Stennis-Owens

A publication of

Eber & Wein Publishing
Pennsylvania

Speaking Freely Part II
Copyright © 2021 by Audra Stennis-Owens

All rights reserved under the International and Pan-American copyright conventions. No part of this book may be reproduced, stored in a retrieval system, or transmitted in any form, electronic, mechanical, or by other means, without written permission of the author.

Library of Congress
Cataloging in Publication Data

ISBN 978-1-60880-695-9

Proudly manufactured in the United States of America by

Eber & Wein Publishing

Pennsylvania

Special Thanks

God
Jessie owens
Lee & Louise Stennis (RIP)
Ruby Lindsey-Jones (RIP)
Kiya, Shaina, Jessica, Simone Owens
Andre Stennis
Linda Jones
Stanley Jones
Ann Stennis Blake
The Lindsey Family
The Stennis Family
Rodney Nichols
Stephanie Smith-Barnes
Karenina Smith & the Smith Family
Deacon Bill Hampton
Judy Burk (RIP)

To all my family and friends for continually supporting me, buying my books and giving me great feedback… Thank you from the bottom of my heart!

Contents

Part I—Messages from My Soul 1
The Shadows of Nightfall 3
The Code 4
Blend In 6
Family Ties 7
A# Sharp 8
Upside Down 9
Bittersweet 10
The Legend of Love 11
Time to Shine 12
Be Still, My Child 13
We Made Love in the Forest 14
If We Were All Green 15
Sweet Brown Sugar 16
Come Follow Me 17
Words 18
The Mystery of Love 19
Free 20
A Few Good Men 21
Unity 22
Better Than Cornbread 23
When the Sheets Would Come 24
Only the Ocean 26
Free Spirit 27
The Ultimate Betrayal 28

Part II—Say It Out Loud 31
Sister-Cousin 32
The Test of Life 34
The Vampire Slaves 36
Can We Grow Old Together? 37
Slow Down 38
Black Velvet 39
Everything under the Sun 40
The River Is Overflowing 41
Dreaming of You 42
Keep It Moving 43
We Shake It 44
Does Size Matter? 45
Are You Crazy? 46
Hold On 47
Tasty 48
Somewhere over My Rainbow 49
He Don't Love Her 50
She Is Sweet 51
Reversal of Racism 52

Part I

Messages from My Soul

Speaking Freely Part II

The Shadows of Nightfall

The spirits follow me in my dreams
and I wrestled with torment
when I tried to hug my mother
as she shoved money into my hand

I begged the sleep gods not to wake me up
I didn't want to wake up

I wanted to hold my mother real tight
and never let her go

But the shadow lifted
and she was gone
One tear traveled slowly down my face

I didn't cry out
just laid in bed
trying hard to interpret what my mother wanted
as my dream lingered in my thoughts

I'll wait…until she returns to me
in another dream

(A tribute to my mother, Annie L. Stennis)

Audra Stennis-Owens

The Code

You know the code
the one that our ancestors/tribe/natives
left us

Signature stamp
the order process for survival

They didn't write it on paper
It was etched in our minds
told to us at a young age
with reminders of the process
as we moved up the ladder
to engage in the circle of our heritage

how to live
who to stay away from and the reasons

The cry of the spirits
when to cut our hair…on the growing moon
the strength
the homemade remedies, herbs, spices
for health, love, and prosperity
transformation of medicine from the earth
(Lizzie Lindsey's tea remedy for colds and sickness)

Speaking Freely Part II

Warnings from God
the protection
the insight of life and death
through the tunnel of dreams
the code handed down through our family tree
our blended culture
long kept secrets to our circle
only to pass to the ones who enter our realm
We grow from their strength

*(Dedicated to my grandmother and mother,
Ruby and Louise and the Lindsey family)*

Audra Stennis-Owens

Blend In

I can't blend in
because of the skin I'm in
can't take a back seat
because my color is unique

I am black from Africa
I am red from America
I am white from Europe
I am made from God

There is no place for pain
no time to hate
"so please stop!"
for God's sake

I can't blend in
because you don't like my hue
so just accept me...
like I
accept you!

Speaking Freely Part II

Family Ties

We have added and multiplied
like God told us to do in the Bible

Our family flows freely like branches
on a giant tree
worldwide and with wide eyes
generations are flying free like birds flying south

We have subtracted
as death departed our loved ones away
and our family legends have lived on
through our offspring

We cling to the memories
like babies cradled in their mothers' arms
safe and secure
as we carry traits of our ancestors
and offer the same respect
our parents taught us to display throughout our lives

And our family tree
will continue to grow
abundantly forever in history

A# Sharp

I am A# Sharp
music in your hands

You play my cords
You hum my thoughts

I am A# Sharp
My melody comes out
and every time you touch me
my insides sing with whimsical excitement

I am A# Sharp
naked on your grandstaff
generating tunes of love
You control the rhythm

A song is born
in the key of love

Speaking Freely Part II

Upside Down

I know I'm standing upside down
because crazy things are happening all around

Hatred
Mass shootings
Lies
Murder
Theft
Political shame and unrest
The nasty pandemic of 2020 called COVID-19

I mean clearly
I feel the rush
of blood to my head

I'm spinning
and I'm not even dreaming
and I am certainly not dead

but the world is literally upside down

Audra Stennis-Owens

Bittersweet

It's great to know
that you
can't hurt me
because I have God on my side

You can't disrespect me
reject me
lie to me
abuse me
fool me
or anything else you had planned

But it is bittersweet
to know that
the snake in you
has revealed its ugly head
and your days have turned black

(A note for bullies at work)

Speaking Freely Part II

The Legend of Love

I never knew you could fall in love so deeply
like a flower rooted in the ground
holding so firm

Love feels that way
the stay of power

heart pounding
while your insides squeeze
life into love

as your mind is awakened
to what will come
feelings that you can't explain

desire
wanting to give into
the passion

Love will take you places
love will leave you speechless
and love will make you submit

Your eyes will open wide
like the clouds so the rain can escape

Your body will relax like a river
flowing gently
over odd-shaped rocks

Love will make you grip the universe!

Audra Stennis-Owens

Time to Shine

Sit up straight
smile
relax
free your mind
be cool
be happy
be free as a jaybird
take a deep breath
and live life to the fullest
because we only have one

So it's time to shine!

Speaking Freely Part II

Be Still, My Child

Don't move
Don't grow up
I want to see my masterpiece God made

Your face
your beauty
and your electric smile . . .
stay little
so I can hold you for a while

My precious baby
I watched you all the days of your life
so don't grow up
and I'll try not to cry

Like a treasure
I'll keep you wrapped in my arms
protecting you forever with love
keeping you safe from any harm

(Dedicated to my baby girl Simone Owens)

Audra Stennis-Owens

We Made Love in the Forest

To the beat of drums
we interrupted the forest
Leaves rustled
the wind blew
as my lover's nature grew

As we used the trees like furniture
but we did not cut the wood
as we made the space our sanctuary

Our hearts beat rapidly
as the dear danced
lizards laughed
frogs jumped
birds chirped
and a baby bear blushed in the distance nearby
I enjoyed the soft breeze
and lifted my eyes to the sky

We made haste
to taste the flavor of our folly
as my lover beat the drum
with wicked percussion
It's like he read my mind
and saw my vision
He took hold of my body
and made love to me
with critical rhythmic precision

Speaking Freely Part II

If We Were All Green

If we were all green
Would you judge me?
Would you give me the promotion?
Would you deny me that bank loan?
Would you give me fair medical treatment?

And if we were all green
Would you follow me around in the store?
Would you stop me in traffic?
Would you assume I was a thief?
Would you laugh at me?

And if we were all green
Would you still try and kill me?
Would you lie on me?
Would you try and put me in a category?

Audra Stennis-Owens

Sweet Brown Sugar

My brown sugar is so sweet
just like you like it . . .

round hips
nothing added
nothing fake
nothing bought
and nothing padded

all natural
from Mother Earth
nothing but sweet brown sugar
up under this here skirt

Come Follow Me

Come and follow me
under the sun
grinning at nature
breathing pot belly hot air

as the heat
moves over our flesh

We will take a journey . . .
our secret
no one else
just you and me

The warm sun will taste our skin
we will giggle
and we will grin

lay under the trees
capture the moment
and savor a soft melancholy breeze

Audra Stennis-Owens

Words

Despite your nasty words and lies
it was the dirty look
within your devilish eyes

They gave the evil in your heart away
the same look you carry
darn near every blink of day

But when you opened your mouth
foolishness and ignorance
always seemed to seep out

You poor, stupid soul . . .
you'll be a dumb, bumbling fool
until you grow old

Speaking Freely Part II

The Mystery of Love

When you gaze excites me
when your touch teases me
when your hugs warm me
when your kiss surprises me
when you love me deeply . . .
with sweet amazing harmony

Audra Stennis-Owens

Free

The day you can walk away
from something or someone sour
make a change
and have your own power

Call your own shots
and not work a nine-to-five
Have strength and peace
and don't put up with no jive!

Have the ability to walk on the wild side
and just be completely free
to travel far
from the land to the sea

To close your eyes
blink and think fast
to erase all bad memories and bad people
dangling in your present or past

Speaking Freely Part II

A Few Good Men

I picked you out
because of your nature
and to talk about

your ethics
your honesty
and your ability to be true men . . .
men who never change

You are godly men
praying men
You have wisdom
You are protectors and providers
You wear the whole armor of God
You seek God's favor
You are true to your loyalty

I recognize you through the years
of what I have seen among men

You have not been swayed
by foolishness
by any person, man, or woman
by money or material objects
by ungodly demons
You have not let the devil beguile you…Selah

These words I say in honor of a few good men

*(Dedicated to Jessie Owens, Andre Stennis, Rodney Nichols
and Deacon Bill Hampton)*

Audra Stennis-Owens

Unity

The vows we say
are sacred in our hearts
The rings we wear
are the circle of our unity
as we do our part

But it's the love we share
which holds true
as we join together

So we will walk with the Lord
in each step we take
and He will walk with us
in every decision we make

As we finalize our marriage
with a kiss
with family and friends
we'll celebrate with bliss

Speaking Freely Part II

Better Than Cornbread

The way you buttered me up
was better than cornbread

I didn't have greens
no delicate tender meat

just your words
straight out of Heaven
and oh boy
were they sweet . . .

I embraced your words
with my anxious ears
hung on each word
brought my eyes to tears

Now I'm hooked on you
because
by far
you are better than cornbread

Audra Stennis-Owens

When the Sheets Would Come

Dark into the night
as black souls slept lightly
restless at best
sweat poured from exhausted bodies
as the old shack was hot
from the heckled woods

Whispers of death
a pinch away
as trees stood tall
adorned with old bloody ropes, a stench of hatred

One eye open
and one foot on the floor
God forbid
if the sheets burst through the door

The horses were the security alarm
back in those days
as the horse's shoes slapped the ground
a warning for black souls
to take cover and remove floor boards
and get down below
under the house, close to the dirt

Speaking Freely Part II

As the sheets entered the old shack
no sign of the black bodies were found
frozen with fear
they didn't dare make a sound
as they held their breath
while waiting underground

When the sheets road away
black souls emerged
cried out
and thanked God to see another day

All the demons behind the sheets
passed their hatred on to their offspring
and God punished them all
with mental and physical pain . . . and death!

Audra Stennis-Owens

Only the Ocean

The water won't tell
as it gently flows
over our warm bodies
of the secrets we created there

The sparkle in our eyes
as we love each other lavishly
holding each other
as if there was no tomorrow

But tomorrow came the next day
as we slept
under the radiant sky

but the ocean won't tell
as we balance our secrets

Speaking Freely Part II

Free Spirit

Come down here
and kiss my soul
as the sky turns red
with the sun's mighty power

I offer you the strength
of the guiding light

as we breathe freely
into love
like the ocean caressing sand

I softly whisper,
"Come down here and kiss my soul!"

Audra Stennis-Owens

The Ultimate Betrayal

Is this how you show me your love?
Is it, brother?
By dragging my name through the mud

Family is thought to be forever
but you fooled me
You talked about me real bad
and, boy, you were so darn clever

So many people came to me with your words
but they didn't believe you anyway

I thought we had each other's back
but when I turned around
you hit me with a whack!
and you let a she devil get you off track

the same one you were trying to get rid of
when you talked about her and her family
But you took the car she bought you
and ate the food she cooked for you

Just think . . . I kept all of your secrets
while you were doing your dirt
playing mind games
with all kinds of young and old skirts

Speaking Freely Part II

Had ladies coming to my house
about your lies
while I tried to figure your junk out
standing confused
promising yourself to someone else
but still I didn't betray you
No words ever came out of my mouth

Used my car and didn't fill it up with gas
wouldn't even fix the flat tire
Even let you borrow money that you never paid back
You forgot everything I did for you . . . everything from the past
Never even apologized
Do you really love me, brother?

Or are you still wearing that betrayal mask?

(To all the people who shared stories of betrayal with me

Part II

Say It Out Loud

Audra Stennis-Owens

Sister-Cousin

Swaddled by the country life
dry, hot southern dreams
as we, De Havilland and I, played
and gazed at fluffy fields

Summertime meant fun
and running wild in nature
all while watching out for deadly snakes

Those summer days
to have my sister-cousin all to myself

As we enjoyed homemade biscuits
figs, fresh vegetables
milk from the cows
and meat from the smokehouse

The taste of fried chicken
a result of the killing from the farm

And the love from my sister-cousin
our southern roots
same values
same way of thinking
our love for God
as memories rewind back to the baths by the fire
in the old wash tub
water bought up from the spring

Speaking Freely Part II

Close as close can be
comfort for my heart by my sister-cousin
secrets of truth of the past
making memories
happy ones
and the love that will forever last

The memory on Ohio Street in Omaha, Nebraska
the bite from the rat
reflections from the sixties

All grown up
we both married
I stayed in Omaha
my cousin moved to Canada
but that didn't keep us apart

As the old black telephone
kept me in close touch with her
we never stopped writing letters . . .
letters that I cherished

As the airplane played taxi
to our long-distance visits

You truly loved me in my youth
and as we both grew older
my love never stopped for my sister-cousin . . .
until death parted me from you

*(Words from Louise's Mouth, told by Louise's daughter,
Audra Stennis-Owens)*

Audra Stennis-Owens

The Test of Life

We are born into the world naked
We are clothed by our mothers
and fed until we can feed ourselves
and walk and talk
She unwinds her strings and sends you off to school
were you are sometimes bullied
taught to read, write and do outrageous math problems
sometimes lunch or gym class is your favorite part of your day

then you bounce into your teenage years
where you make decisions to be obedient or dis-obedient
listen in class
play sports, be in a choir, or school plays
decide whether you will try knew fads or not
pick out a school crush …
kiss them and graduate

then you enter into your young adult years
make love for the first time… like it, and keep doing it
get a job or go to college
so you can introduce yourself to every bill known to man
carry the debt like a pregnant women
get a greater job
and establish more debt…
only to realize that it wasn't worth it

Speaking Freely Part II

sometimes you marry your lover
have children and buy a house
buy many cars . . . while you watch them lose their value

Step into parenthood gone mad
drive your children all over the city
buy all kinds of clothes they only wear for a hot second
then release them onto the floor of their rooms
and show off their attitudes

You watch your offspring leave home for their futures
You call or text to check on them
They carry on with life and soon you're a grandparent

Finally you spend quality time with your husband or wife
spend money like you want to
live a little more . . . like it
make a to-do list
and wait for God to give you further instructions

Audra Stennis-Owens

The Vampire Slaves

"Could they exist in this error?"

They are not dead
cynical
but it's not in my head

Hated like poison dirt
because of black and brown and red skin

But behold
they sprang up out of the earth

They could read and write
and they knew how to disappear
out of anyone's sight
They were smart as they hung from trees
but they woke in the darkness
to hunt their evil prey in the middle of the night

Vampire slaves move quietly
across tainted interrupted lands
blood buried deep under the soil of ancestors
who were mistreated, raped, and killed

But here's the twist . . .
the vampires are the offspring of the dead
You don't know who they are
or where they roam
when they will feed on the evil-doers

You only know they do exist

Speaking Freely Part II

Can We Grow Old Together?

Can we kiss under the moonlight?

Like we did in our youth
remembering the laughs
the playful times
pleasant talk
and planning our future

Can we cook those same easy meals for two?

When the grocery bill was only thirty-five dollars,
and the groceries lasted about two weeks

Can we travel to those same spots?

The spots where we made memories
and collected souvenirs,
the souvenirs that now collect dust

Can we make love?

Without any interruption
from kids, dogs, or telephone calls
in every room in the house

Can we pray together?

In good or bad times
keeping our faith strong

Can we grow old together?

Slow Down

Don't rush through life . . . slow down
Cherish and obey your parents
Spend time and kiss your grandmother
Learn from the elders
Tell your family you love them
Protect and love your mate, deeply

Call that friend
Use your God-given talents
Praise and thank God every day
Pray daily

Rewind your thoughts
and think of good memories
Write a journal about your life
because life goes by fast

Slow down
and enjoy all the great things
God has to offer

"Please, slow down!"

(Dedicated to our youth)

Speaking Freely Part II

Black Velvet

Black Velvet
was his flavor
She was something he wanted to savor

Black Velvet
was his passion
He wanted to keep her laughing

Black Velvet
was his muse
He wanted to follow all her crazy rules

Black Velvet
drove him wild
like dangling candy
in front of an anxious frisky child

Audra Stennis-Owens

Everything under the Sun

Love and laughter
the beauty of the earth

Life and death
God's choice

The good, the bad, and the ugly
a whole lot of ugly

Food and hunger
hopeless and homeless

Dreams of hope
prosperity hanging in the balance

Lies and lust
wasted space

New technology
but drive-in movies are gone with the wind

Priceless thoughts
and books still linger on

Money travels
and criminals roam free

The seasons are unpredictable now . . .
but God is still in charge

The River Is Overflowing

Like salt in my eyes
I can't believe the burn on the box
They call it television

I call it the eyeball to hatred
at an all-time high
and everybody's blood has turned black
and it's 2020
but the time machine is headed in the wrong direction . . .
backwards

And evil-doers are jumping on
like bandits robbing a train, straight to hell

And everybody is ignoring everything
that God spoke about
love, respect, morals
everything in the bible

The river is overflowing
and there is a flood of death brewing

Don't get caught in the flood!

Audra Stennis-Owens

Dreaming of You

Your face
your hair
your scent
your skin
and your warm caress
all the things that make me grin

Your touch
your hugs
soft words in my ears
a love that will last
in our golden years

Your heart
your soul
I'll love you forever
until we age and grow old

Speaking Freely Part II

Keep It Moving

For those who hate you
for those who lie on you
for those who disrespect you
for those who betray you
for those who put the knife in your back
and twist it
and twist it

forgive them
and keep it moving!

Audra Stennis-Owens

We Shake It

Oh, let that tune play
It sends a signal to my ears
gets me to my feet
My hips wake up
and I shake it to the beat

The soul music is so good
Bodies start to move
When the beat thumps harder
everyone starts to groove

We shake it so good
it's in our ancestry
sounds and moves from Africa
traveling down through history

We cannot hide
what we feel
the vibrations in our bones
you better believe it's real

We shake it
because the music
won't let us be still

Speaking Freely Part II

Does Size Matter?

"Does your size matter?"
Hell yes
the size of your brain!

If you are stupid—goodbye
If you don't work—goodbye
If you are not a man of God—goodbye

If you have no manners—goodbye
If you are a player—goodbye
If you love a life of crime
baby
I don't have time

"Does size matter?" Hell yes!

(For men)

Audra Stennis-Owens

Are You Crazy?

Do you call him twelve times a day?
Do you follow him?
Do you search his phone and pockets?
Do you keep him from his family?
Do you assume things with no evidence at all?
Do you start a fight for no good reason?
Do you accuse him of something you made up in your head?

Are you crazy?
Yes you are
It's called stalker

(To women)

Speaking Freely Part II

Hold On

Wait
hold on
I'm not ready
It's my first time
so slow down

No
never did that before
You can't touch that
I can't allow you to
because this is mine and I control this

I have to speak up
My mom told me to be bold

Sorry, but you can't move in!
My heart is on the line

Tasty

It's amazing
Call me crazy
"But isn't love so very tasty?"

It's interesting
somewhat appetizing
You hunger for it
that makes it surprising

It's got flavor
and it's physically attracting
Wait for it . . .
because it's always very distracting

It's free, no money involved
but you pay Cupid's cost
Mentally out of control
you can and will get lost

It can begin with a simple kiss
or an innocent crush
Savory words and magical bliss
brings on that tasty rush

"Isn't Love Tasty?"

Speaking Freely Part II

Somewhere over My Rainbow

Somewhere over my rainbow
I'll have it all—
sweet peace and joy
and a tranquil waterfall

a beautiful blue sky
and large green trees
little bitty birds
that sit and sing to me

passion and true love
and a giant pot of gold
a warm embrace
and my lover's hand to hold

No pain, no hatred
and love bursting at the seems
just happiness and joy
and mountains of fairytale dreams

Audra Stennis-Owens

He Don't Love Her

Like a snake
he slithered her way
stole her treasure
left his seed
and then ran off to play

He's a bad boy
with good looks
but rather dumb
can't even comprehend the words in a book

He don't love her
'cause love is respected
and his behavior is flawed
her love and his baby
he walked away from and rejected!

She Is Sweet

She is very sweet
like cotton candy on the tip of the tongue

Her voice soft and tender
like a whispering breeze

She is beautiful
like a doll with soft brown eyes

funny and enchanting
like a princess in a storybook

Her style is graceful
like a ballerina

Her words are soothing
to the listening ear

Her story . . . she is sweet

Audra Stennis-Owens

Reversal of Racism

Image being snatched from your country
and riding a ship to another country
where you are raped, sold, and separated from your family
whipped and treated less than a dog

Image putting money in a bank
only to go back to that same bank
and be told you don't have any

Image having your house burned to the ground
because of your skin color
Image being spit on

Image someone calling you a name
and hating you
but you take the time to keep coming to rape them
"If you hate them, why touch them?"

Image being segregated on another part of land
away from people who hate you
but they keep coming to your side
to disturb your life
"If you hate them, then stay away from them?"

Image your great-grandmother and -grandfather being approached
by an old white man
to warn them
that he heard four young white men
plotting to rape your beautiful daughters
while they walked home from school the next day
(Lizzie and Noah were thankful for the warning)

Speaking Freely Part II

Image moving to Omaha, Nebraska
in the nineteen sixties
going to the Old Brandies building downtown
to a food shop, asking for an application for a job
only to be taken to the kitchen
with your friend
as you both stood there for hours
and no one said a word to you
so you left

Image buying a house
in a mixed neighborhood
Blacks, Jews, Native American, bi-racial, white
later to discover that the deed to your house
reads: No Jews, Negroes, or Indians can purchase the house

Image your boyfriend's ninety-year-old uncle
telling you in the nineteen eighties
about the time he saw his best friend's father
hanging from a tree in Mississippi
as they walked home from school

Now Image working jobs
where nobody who looks like you
can get a supervisor or manager position
or never be able to move to other positions

Image getting laid off
and the people called in the office are brown
and you ask why us
only to be told, I can't tell you
and still have to turn around and
train the people who will replace you

Audra Stennis-Owens

Imagine having a college education
and being offered a job on the phone
and then you get there
and the person who assured you of the job
won't even shake your hand
and tell you that the job has been filled

Now image when you leave the house
and you get pulled over
only to get a ticket for something you didn't do
or get SHOT DEAD BECAUSE OF YOUR COLOR
AND YOU HAD YOUR HANDS UP
AND YOU DIDN'T HAVE A WEAPON
AND YOU HAD LITTLE KIDS IN THE CAR
AND YOU DIE
AND LIES ARE TOLD ABOUT YOU
AND THE PEOPLE WHO CAUSED YOUR DEATH
GET A PAID LEAVE
AND THEN GET THEIR JOBS BACK
AND THEN TURN AROUND
AND THEY KEEP DOING THE SAME THING!

NOW IMAGE PEOPLE WITH WHITE SKIN
GOING THROUGH THIS
ALL THE TIME!

TURN THE TABLES
"DO YOU UNDERSTAND NOW!"
WHAT YOU DO IN THE DARK
REMEMBER THE CAMERAS ARE ALWAYS ROLLING NOW
BUT REMEMBER, GOD IS ALWAYS WATCHING
AND THOUGH YOU THINK YOU WILL GET AWAY
GOD HELP YOU BECAUSE GOD WILL HAND DOWN YOUR
PUNISHMENT

CPSIA information can be obtained
at www.ICGtesting.com
Printed in the USA
LVHW092127170921
698073LV00003B/147